What Is the U.S. Constitution?

Joanne Randolph

Rosen
REAL
READERS

Rosen Classroom Books & Materials
New York

Published in 2003 by The Rosen Publishing Group, Inc.
29 East 21st Street, New York, NY 10010

Book Design: Ron A. Churley

Photo Credits: Cover, pp. 1, 7 (insets), 10–11, 12–13 © Hulton/Archive; pp. 4–5, 16 (inset) © Joseph Sohm/Corbis; pp. 4 (inset), 8–9, 12 (inset), 18–19, 19 (inset) © Bettmann/Corbis; p. 9 (inset) © Gary Randall/ FPG International; p. 11 (inset) by Jessica Livingston; pp. 14–15 © Andrea Pistolesi/The Image Bank; p. 15 (inset) © Wally McNamee/Corbis; pp. 16–17 © Jurgen Vogt/The Image Bank; pp. 20–21 © David Gould/The Image Bank; p. 21 (left inset) © Jacques M. Chenet/Corbis; p. 21 (right inset) © Reuters NewMedia Inc./Corbis; p. 22 © Topham/The Image Works.

ISBN: 0-8239-6393-4
6-pack ISBN: 0-8239-9581-X

Manufactured in the United States of America

Contents

What Is a Constitution?   5

Creating Laws for a New Nation   6

Lessons from History   10

The U.S. Constitution   14

The Bill of Rights   18

The Living Constitution   20

Guarding Our Constitution   22

Glossary   23

Index   24

4

What Is a Constitution?

You may have heard people talk about the U.S. **Constitution**, but you may not have known what it was. A constitution tells what kind of government and laws a nation will have. It lists the powers and duties of the government, and the rights of the people.

The leaders who wrote the U.S. Constitution worked hard to make the best system of rules they could. Our Constitution is special because it allows all American citizens to have a say in how the U.S. government is run. It protects the rights of all American people. Today, this system of government is called a **democracy**.

The original U.S. Constitution is on display at the National Archives Building in Washington, D.C. More than a million people come to view this historic American document every year.

Creating Laws for a New Nation

In 1783, the colonies in America won their freedom from England and became the United States of America. The new nation's leaders had to decide what kind of government to set up. They created the first system of government with the **Articles of Confederation**.

In this system, each state was like a small country. States had power over their own affairs. They could tax their citizens and even print their own money. The national government had very little power over the states.

By 1785, it became clear that the Articles of Confederation were not enough to hold the young nation together. Many leaders quickly realized that the new nation would not last without a national government that had the power to make decisions for the good of all the states.

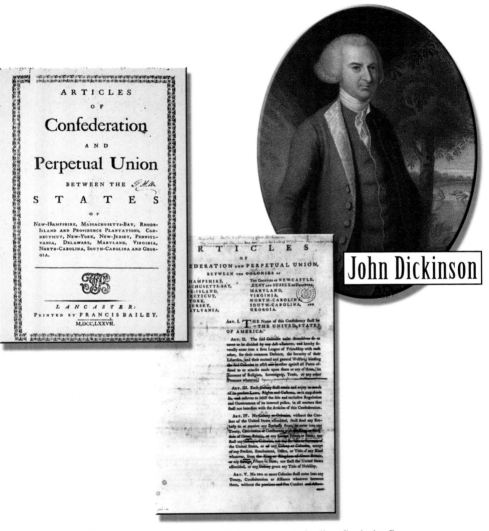

John Dickinson

A man named John Dickinson wrote the first draft of the Articles of Confederation. He had been governor of Delaware from 1781 to 1782, and governor of Pennsylvania from 1782 to 1785.

In 1787, leaders from twelve of the thirteen states met in Philadelphia, Pennsylvania, to make changes in the Articles of Confederation. During this meeting, there were many disagreements. Finally, they decided that it would be better to write a new constitution.

The leaders **debated** for many months over what to put in the new constitution. Some wanted to have a strong national government. Others were afraid that a national government with too much power would not treat all the states fairly.

Leaders from large states said that their states should have more say in how the national government was run because they had more people. Leaders from small states argued that all states should have an equal say.

Independence Hall

Rhode Island did not send any men to the meeting. The other twelve states elected seventy-four leaders to go to the meeting, but only fifty-five went. The leaders met in Independence Hall in Philadelphia.

Lessons from History

To help them write the new constitution, American leaders studied two very old constitutions. One was created hundreds of years ago by the Iroquois (EAR-uh-kwoy) League, a group of six Native American nations. Under the rules made for the League, each nation had the right to make laws for its own people, but the League made decisions on matters that concerned all the nations. The League was governed by a **council** made up of leaders from all the nations. Leaders were chosen by the people, and they had to work together to make plans that everyone agreed on.

The Mohawk, Oneida, Onondaga, Cayuga, and Seneca nations formed the Iroquois League more than 400 years ago. The Tuscarora nation joined the League in the early 1700s.

American leaders wanted the different states to have a say in how they were ruled, just like the nations of the Iroquois League. Each state has leaders chosen by the people who help make laws for the good of all Americans. This way, every state gets a say in how they are ruled.

Iroquois Council

11

American leaders also looked at the Magna Carta (MAG-nuh KAHR-tuh), a constitution written in England in 1215 and signed by King John. It said that everyone, even the king, had to obey the law. It also said that the king would not have all the power. He had to share power with other government leaders.

Many Americans were worried that a single leader for the U.S. would have too much power, just like an English king. American leaders took a lesson from the Magna Carta. They decided to make a government of three parts that would have to share power. That way, no one person or part would have too much power.

The Latin words "*Magna Carta*" mean "Great Charter." Many countries besides the United States used the Magna Carta as a model for their own governments.

The U.S. Constitution

On September 17, 1787, American leaders finally agreed on a Constitution that satisfied everyone. They created a national government with three branches, or parts. The first branch, **Congress**, makes laws for the whole country. Congress is made up of the House of **Representatives** and the Senate.

Both the House of Representatives and the Senate are made up of government leaders **elected** by the people of each state. In the Senate, each state has equal say because each state has two senators. In the House of Representatives, states with more people get to elect more representatives. This means they have more say in how the House is run.

Every year, about 3 million people visit the Capitol Building in Washington, D.C. Visitors can attend meetings of Congress and listen to the debates about laws.

House of Representatives

The second branch of the government—the president—is elected by the people of the United States. The president runs the government and has the final say on laws made by Congress.

The third branch of government is the **Supreme Court**. The judges of the Supreme Court make sure that local, state, and national governments follow the laws of the U.S. Constitution. Judges are chosen by the president and serve on the Supreme Court for life.

U.S. Constitution

The Constitution also says that the people have a say in how the government is run. The people elect the president, senators, and representatives. A government that allows the people to elect the leaders who run the government is called a **republic**.

The president and his family live in the White House. The White House is in Washington, D.C.

The Bill of Rights

Before the Constitution became law, it had to be approved by nine of the thirteen states. This happened on June 21, 1788.

Many people did not want to approve the Constitution because it did not say anything about the rights of the people. The leaders agreed to write some **amendments**, or changes, to add to the Constitution. They wrote ten amendments that listed rights the government cannot take away from the people. These include the right to say what you think and the right to belong to the church of your choice. These ten amendments, called the **Bill of Rights**, became law on December 15, 1791.

The Bill of Rights is one of the most important things ever written in our nation's history. Our country would be very different today if the Constitution did not have this promise to guard people's rights and freedom.

The Living Constitution

The leaders who wrote our Constitution were wise men. They realized that as the country grew and changed, there would need to be changes in the Constitution. They made sure that it would always be possible to make changes. They also made sure the changes would be fair by requiring that most people agree to the changes before they could become law.

Voting for leaders and laws is one of our most important rights and duties.

The fact that we can change the Constitution when we need to has helped to make it strong. The power to make changes has helped us to create a fair society. For example, changes in the Constitution made **slavery** illegal. Other changes gave women the right to vote. Our country is much stronger because the Constitution can grow and change with us.

Guarding Our Constitution

One story says that after the leaders had finished writing our Constitution, a man asked Benjamin Franklin what kind of government they had given us. The story says that Franklin replied, "A republic—if you can keep it."

Franklin meant that the people must do their part to keep the country strong. The Constitution gives us many rights. It also gives us many **responsibilities**. Good government does not depend only on a nation's leaders. It also depends on the people who elect them.

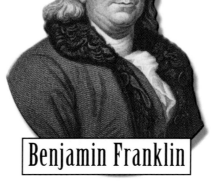

Benjamin Franklin

Glossary

amendment An official change.

Articles of Confederation The first set of rules for the U.S. government. It was replaced by the U.S. Constitution in 1788.

Bill of Rights The first ten amendments to the U.S. Constitution, which list the rights of the citizens.

Congress The branch of U.S. government that makes our laws. Congress is made up of two groups: the Senate and the House of Representatives.

constitution The basic rules of a country or state.

council A group called together to give advice and to discuss or settle questions.

debate To argue or discuss.

democracy A system of government that is run, directly or indirectly, by the people it governs.

elect To choose someone for public office by voting for him or her.

representative Someone who acts in place of others.

republic A form of government whose leader or leaders are elected to office.

responsibility Something that a person must take care of or complete.

slavery The unfair system of being "owned" by and having to work for someone else.

Supreme Court The part of the U.S. government that makes sure everyone follows the laws of the U.S. Constitution.

Index

A
amendments, 18
Articles of
        Confederation, 6, 8

B
Bill of Rights, 18

C
Congress, 14, 16

D
democracy, 5

E
England, 6, 13

F
Franklin, Benjamin, 22

H
House of
        Representatives,
        14

I
Iroquois League, 10, 11

L
law(s), 5, 10, 11, 13,
        14, 16, 18, 20

M
Magna Carta, 13

P
Philadelphia,
        Pennsylvania, 8
president, 16, 17

R
representatives, 14, 17
republic, 17, 22

S
Senate, 14
senators, 14, 17
Supreme Court, 16